I love

Written and illustrated by
Shoo Rayner

Collins

Brook is afraid of lots of things.
He is afraid of hunting, fishing and getting wet.

He is afraid of flight, too.
"I will help you, Brook," Dad tells him.

Dad hunts in the green lagoon.
"The green lagoon is soaking wet!"
Brook complains.

"Come on, Brook! You might like it!"
Dad tells him.

Eek!

Sploosh!

"I do not like the green lagoon,"
Brook claims. "I love it!"

Dad scoops up a shrimp.

"Yuck! Shrimps!" Brook groans.
"Come on! You might like them!"
Dad tells Brook.

Brook scoops up a shrimp from the soft, brown mud.

Scoop!

"I do not like shrimps," Brook snorts.
"I love them!"

Slurp!

Gulp!

Yum!

Dad and Brook creep up a steep cliff.

Dad flaps off. Brook looks down.

Brook shivers in fright.

"I am afraid!" he wails.

"Come on! You might like it!"
Dad tells Brook.

Brook flaps. Then he swoops and floats on the wind.

Yippee! This is the best fun ever!

"Dad," hoots Brook. "I do not like flight ... I love it!"

Brook's flight

15

Review: After reading

Use your assessment from hearing the children read to choose any GPCs, words or tricky words that need additional practice.

Read 1: Decoding

- Encourage the children to practise reading words that contain two or three syllables.
  - Point to **hunting** on page 2. Ask the children to sound out and blend each "chunk" or syllable. (*h/u/n/t – i/ng*)
  - Repeat for: page 3 **afraid** (*a – f/r/ai/d*); page 4 **lagoon** (*l/a – g/oo/n*); page 11 **shivers** (*sh/i/v – er/s*)

Read 2: Prosody

- Model reading each page with expression to the children.
- After you have read each page, ask the children to have a go at reading with expression.
- Read the book again, with you reading Dad's spoken words and the children reading Brook's.

Read 3: Comprehension

- Turn to pages 14 and 15 and ask the children to retell the story in their own words using the pictures linked with arrows as prompts.
- For every question ask the children how they know the answer. Ask:
  - On page 5, do you think Brook will change during this story? In what ways? (e.g. *he will learn to be less afraid*; *he will love flying*)
  - On page 9, what has Brook discovered so far? (*He has discovered that he loves the lagoon and he loves shrimps.*)
  - On pages 10 and 11, why do you think Brook and Dad climb the cliff? (e.g. *so they can fly off the top*; *so Brook can learn to fly*)
  - On page 12, how do you think Brook is feeling now? (e.g. *He is happy and excited.*)